Record of Dissent

Poems of Protest in an Authoritarian Age

The Chaos Section Poetry Project
Austin, TX

2025

Cover Artwork:
June 14th by Bonner Fowles (acrylic on canvas)
Interior Artwork:
Creative Resistance by Phoebe Shade (digital/mixed media illustration)
Editor: Nick Allison
Editorial Consultants:
Rachel Armes-McLaughlin, Meridith Allison

ISBN: 979-8-9993042-0-9

First published: Summer 2025

Published by: The Chaos Section Press
Austin, Texas

thechaossectionpoetryproject.com

Dedication

For every artist who uses their talent and skill to fight injustice, defend truth, and speak for the unheard.

*"Not everything that is faced can be changed,
but nothing can be changed until it is faced."*

— James Baldwin

*"Poetry is what happens when words are opened up,
and those worlds within are made visible."*

— Jeff Tweedy, *How to Write One Song*

This collection was created to amplify voices of dissent and reflection. All contributors retain full rights to their work and were not charged or compensated.

This print edition is offered at or near production cost to help offset publishing expenses. A free, digital version of this book is also available to read or download at thechaossectionpoetryproject.com.

Thank you for respecting the spirit of this project and the work of the authors included here.

Table of Contents

Letter from the Editor

It's rare that I write with an actual pen and paper these days, but that's what I'm doing now. I refuse to bring a laptop to a place like this—and my rucksack doesn't have room for a MacBook anyway. I'm sitting beside a stream on the lower stretch of the Chasm Lake Trail in Rocky Mountain National Park. The water moves quick and clear over rounded stones, fed by snowmelt higher up. Longs Peak rises off to my right, partially hidden by trees but unmistakable in its shape. To my left, the forest thins and the ground begins to slope into a wide field scattered with boulders. I was lucky enough to see an elk herd this morning—the big beasts moving far too gracefully for something their size. But I'm far enough off the main roads and trailheads now that I haven't seen another human in hours. It's 72 and sunny. There's a south wind, and the only sounds beyond the scratching of my pen on paper are decidedly not made by people.

It's peaceful here. A much-needed solo trip through one of the most beautiful national parks this country has to offer. One could almost forget what's happening across the rest of it right now. I haven't seen the news today, but yesterday Trump mobilized a battalion of Marines from 29 Palms—along with the National Guard units he'd already activated—to shut down immigration protests in Los Angeles. Part of me wonders if this is the tipping point. Surely everyone can recognize the authoritarian vibes in using active-duty military against American citizens. Not that we haven't been heading down this road for months.

Tomorrow I'll hike back out, check the news, and hope I don't have to rewrite this entire introduction because martial law was declared while I was in the mountains and the world is on fire.

Ever since Trump took office in January of 2025, we've been watching the slide. Of course, it started long before that—during his last term—culminating in his incitement of a violent attempt to overturn the 2020 election. But that was just the warm-up. Since returning to office, he's wasted no time escalating.

From mass pardons for Capitol insurrectionists, to the demonization of immigrants, to the rollback of protections that once kept federal agents out of schools, hospitals, and churches. From agents showing up at elementary schools to question immigrant kids without warrants, to sweeping raids that ignored due process and detained people—citizens included. From crackdowns on whistleblowers and journalists, labeling the free press "the enemy of the people," to politicizing federal agencies and issuing executive orders that bypass the courts and Congress. From a Justice Department that acts more like Trump's personal law firm to open defiance of Supreme Court rulings. From purging civil servants under Schedule F to floating a third term with a straight face. From textbook strongman rhetoric to textbook strongman moves.

Legal scholars keep warning that we're fast approaching a constitutional crisis. I think maybe we're already in one.

The idea for this project started to form on November 5th of last year, when it became clear that Donald Trump was going to be elected once again to the presidency. Art and protest have always been linked—here and around the world. Think of Frances Ellen Watkins Harper and Joe Hill. Billie Holiday and Nina Simone. Maya Angelou. Langston Hughes. Audre Lorde. Allen Ginsberg. Woody Guthrie. Bob Dylan. Think of protest signs and graffiti. Of classrooms where kids are still writing poems while their rights and futures are under attack.

When we started pulling this project together, I thought it would be mostly about Trump's return to power. Poems directed at him. Pieces about policy and overreach. And we certainly got some of those. But we also got poems about grief. About trauma. About trying to stay grounded when everything feels unstable.

Some of the work is explicitly political. Some of it is quieter. Some poems are about surviving systems that were never built to support you—being a woman, or disabled, or broke, or trans, or sick in a country that makes those things harder than they need to be. Some are about identity. Some are about burnout. Others don't fit into any one category. But they all show what it feels like to live through this moment. To pay attention. To stay awake. To speak up. To resist the urge to go numb.

The epigraph of this book includes a quote from James Baldwin, who reminded us that not everything we face can be changed—but nothing can be changed until it's faced. That idea stayed with me throughout this project. I'm not expecting this little book of anti-authoritarian poems to change the world, but that's still exactly why we're doing it. Because, as Baldwin also said, "The world changes according to the way people see it, and if you alter, even by a millimeter the way people look at reality, then you can change it."

Maybe one line in one of these poems finds its way to someone who needs it. Maybe it helps them see things a little differently—through the eyes of someone with a different story, a different struggle. Maybe it shifts something—just a millimeter. And maybe that small moment of connection is enough to begin something.

The poems in this book are angry, wounded, proud, desperate, funny, hopeful, and unflinching. They come from poets all over the country—and beyond. Different backgrounds, races, religions, genders, and philosophies. Some have published multiple books. Some have never published anything until now. But they all share something: a love of freedom, a belief in human dignity, and a vision of what this country could be.

They raised their voices—and said in verse what I couldn't say in a hundred more pages of prose. These poets have joined the long tradition of artists speaking out against authoritarianism and abuse.

And if you're reading this book, you're part of that tradition now too.

Onward,
Nick Allison
Colorado
June 10th, 2025

Record of Dissent

They'll Say They Didn't Know

Bartholomew Barker

I can imagine how it feels
to cross a border for a better future and not do the paperwork
to get pregnant and not want to have a baby
to live in a body not carrying the right gender

I can imagine how it feels
to be vilified — to be hunted
to be afraid of every stranger
and some friends

But I'm a straight white man in America
I can't truly understand it in my gut
but I can sympathize

So why then can't I imagine
what caused so many of my fellows
to vote the way they did?

The Gardener

Chris Chan

Someone above our heads is building a fence
to keep his neighbors' weeds out. Pushing the stake
into the ground, he lifts the hammer to strike
the sharp spoke down, and at his feet explodes
a clod of earth. He does this rhythmically — right
fist clenched, left hand loose — as though
the dream of weedless grass were enough
to keep him breathing, to keep him sweating beneath
the springtime sun. The whitewashed wall will leave
no gaps, and the garden he planted will thrive
as it did last season, when no one noticed
the dandelions crouched among the tiger lilies
brought in from elsewhere and now settled
with the rest. Perhaps he thinks the lawn will grow
green again as his rusted shovel sweeps away
another unnamed plant he does not believe
belongs here. Perhaps he wants the simple proof
that this will work out well. Or perhaps it is the truth
of our roots that unsettles him: shallow limbs
interlocking, gnarled arms outstretched, restless as

abandoned kin, dying to flower in full force.

April 18th

Rachel Armes-McLaughlin

The whole world holds its breath.

Who's next to be grabbed off the street
by those in plain clothes with masked identities?

Sent to a prison, a camp, a painful death.

In the 1930s, by train.
But now sent out by air, held aloft by hate.

Sent by air, like the virus they've tried to erase–
not through vaccines, but censorship.

Through scrubbing, but not of hands–
of internet sites, banned books, and lists of dirty words
like diversity, equity, and inclusion.

The whole world holds its breath–
The insanity must end.

Stocked

Chad Parenteau

Our abusers
mourned first,
foremost.

Deathbeds
warmer
than ever.

Gun barrels
loaded,
suckled.

misstra know-it-all

after Stevie Wonder

Matthew E. Henry

he's everything the racists hoped a Black president would be.
a sexual predator, jackal-slinking from one vulgarity
to the next—tiny hands always in someone else's pocket.
a bastard with multiple baby mommas, married—for the moment—
to an off-White woman his supporters used to slut shame, citing
something about "family values." with a bachelor's in shucking,
a master of jiving, he's so crooked he has to screw on his socks—
catching more cases than cold sores, which is surprising considering
the number of prostitutes on his payroll. surrounded by a collection
of shady characters—Dickensian in corruption—he's a study
in ghetto wealth: a bankrupt adept at borrowing money
he's never good for, who thinks gold should adorn everything
his name touches, showers included. he's the most shiftless nigger
I know. and of course he's from New York.

she writes me down

Melissa Lemay

a number on the margins
turns me over and back
i exist in silent
claim numbers

she clack-clack-clacks
hits send to ask
again what year
'the incident' occurred

i tell her i don't remember
most of my life

i list out dates all estimates
in language she probably
does (not) understand,

i understand only incidents
that happened in pennsylvania
qualify me for the aid

new hampshire 1988-1990
sexual abuse by bio father

maryland 2000
pressured into sex acts
with female room mate
at elective course in ancient greek
at johns hopkins university

pennsylvania 2005
dragged into room and
raped by man at party

screamed for help while
parents 'slept' down hall

pennsylvania 2007
raped by different men
coming in and out
apartment window
orchestrated by man
i used pcp with

i throw in a couple abbreviations
she understands abbreviations

Born Naked, the Choice After is Ours

Merril D. Smith

1.
The rot from within festers,
the room reeks,

the lies bloom like corpse flowers,
the stench overwhelming–
it's the new perfume.

Three men in that oval chamber,
only one is a leader,

and I am ashamed.

2.
But—

in the darkness, we open
our eyes, whisper
poetry, till we become
ferocious–

mothers will defend their young,
their young will growl and rise
with spring grass, will march
with ghosts beside them, an army—

remember the beauty,
the red sky of morning,
the coming storm.

clean

Liz Mariani

better get clean before the taxman
comes to tax you for living

i got raped and all i got was this lousy t-shirt

can't teach in america when everywhere is
a classroom ripe for a mass shooting
can't walk/wake/weep in america
when everywhere is a hospital rotten aerosol mustard

i got raped and all i got was this air-raid drill

i don't want your fame or appreciation
your accolades or recognition
your payments or compensations

what i want is to live without the pressure to entertain you
your friends
your friend's friends
your friend's friend's friend's friends

what i want is to live without implication or pressure
to entertain you
to confuse you

to kick up grey and salty dusk dust rust
in the face of a clear sky

i hope you choke on your wanting
the wanting rationalizing
this refracted murder spree
i hope you choke on your wanting
as you traumatize me and everyone i love

Thoughts from the other side of the Mid Atlantic Rift

Sue McBean

Only an ocean away.
On the "scatter my ashes' island.
Across the Atlantic. Rathlin.
Eider ducks coo, tide ebbs and flows,
and oyster catchers scream alarm.

The soft eiders,
huddle close for safety in numbers.
They seem to fly under water.
Menacing gulls circle overhead.
There are no chicks yet
for airborne rats to play tyrant over. They'll
cross the Sound to scavenge easier food,
sharing it with land rats:
chips from waste bins in a seaside town.

In neglected ground the flowers cannot flourish.
Deep tap roots of perennial weeds must be dug up
with fork, sweat and broken back.
And tangled nettle runners traced along their course
dragged out, easier in this drought.
Choking roots in America are not annuals
that pull up with the greatest ease.

Was that the sound of someone going under, in the bay?
A last swoosh of an arm. Drowning.
The panning torch caught sight of a white arm.
It tilted and curved up like a farewell wave, or doff of a cap.
An Eider throwing his head back in silence.

The thick pen, like a chisel,
changes the face of the rock.

Misshapen sculpture replaces
centuries of wisdom, slashes grace and
cuts communities. This installation
grows bigger and more gloomy
with every wound.
The debris of US is swept up and binned.

The wind picks up in the right direction.
At low tide we burn ten years of neglected Hebe hedge.
The flames roar at the base of the bonfire with consuming rage.

The American Dream 2.0

Shannon Frost Greenstein

Part One
In America, we quantize our bodies
and the complexities of our brains –
assigning each part a separate dollar value –
because health insurance companies don't deal in health;
because health insurance companies deal in profit.

In America, we employ thousands
in the manufacture of bulletproof backpacks;
entire factories pumping out Kevlar
like this band-aid is the same thing as a cure.

In America, the Cold War is over,
but our school children are still trained
to *duck and cover* and *fear and pray*,
as if any safety drills are not entirely futile
when the right to bear arms is more sacred
than the right to pursue a future.

In America, we put our architects to work
sketching hostile architecture with each brutal new design.
We exploit the creative left-brain of our brightest citizens
in order to manifest the criminalization of homelessness;
in order to make poverty and mental illness a crime.

In America, we sacrifice our bodies and minds
at the sacred altar of revenue
because *Capitalism was born on the plantation*;
because Matthew Desmond ultimately said it best.

In America, we are scourged by our addiction
to artificial dopamine
and the escape of self-medication,

because the rich just want to be richer;
because oxycodone turns quite the profit.

In America, we are subject to the whims
of Buffet and Bezos and Zuckerberg the Wise;
our corporations stockpile the most finite of resources
like Smaug hoarding the gold of Middle Earth.

In America, we are chasing the nostalgia
of post-WWII opportunities and growth,
because we still have the pressure of our reputation
as the greatest country in the world.

Part Two
In America, our bootstraps are so worn and cracked
that they are no longer subject
to the laws of gravitation;
they no longer support our weight.

In America, we are all battling demons
that haunt us intergenerationally
because our country is vivisected by inequity
and hurt people hurt people.

In America, we are exhausted by minimum wage
and dead-end jobs
and – if we are in the service industry –
we are exhausted from dealing with all your shit.

In America, we are watching the planet melt
in real time and with terrifying detail
because Mother Earth is also exhausted
from dealing with all our shit.

In America, we are pleading for infrastructure –
instead of the most powerful standing military on Earth –
because our military hasn't really been standing;

our military has been fighting incessantly since September 11, 2001.

In America, we go without insulin
and discover our cancers way too late;
we decline out-of-network ambulance rides
because we need that money for bills.

In America, we simply wish our votes mattered
as we bear witness to the stalemate of bipartisanship;
we learn to tolerate the distress of our impotence
amidst the fallout of our democracy.

In America, we are tired of crowd-funding.
In America, we are tired of assault rifles.
In America, we are tired of this Sisyphean fight.
In America, we are just tired.

In America…we all just want The American Dream.

script eighty-five

Liz Mariani

are you are the screenwriter
resting in a field of garlic?

are you are the banker
sinking into another suburban fold?

are you are the lover
at the door on the floor at the door?

are you the border guard?
this is a field of garlic

spin the clearcut field of snow
chew the wind

this is the lack of visibility
this is the best edit

this is snow blindness
this is the cost

How to Dodge Bombs

Patricia J McLean

I think it could be a night like that night in August
just before Utopia got a new wall to replace the broken
falling down, rotten wood wall

Or before the night like that night, or another sort of night altogether
when the broccoli dies of neglect, tomatoes are so heavy vines break
the garden is going to seed anyway so what difference will it make

or maybe it will be the night before or the day before
I will wait for a few more minutes before I leave
and I will still be blocks away

there will be a rumble, a series of popping noises, a column of smoke

Or I could leave earlier and I could be inside at a table already eating
The food is so good there, I could be lifting a glass of wine to my lips
tasting the warmth, smelling summer in it

I could be folded up in blue space and disappear
I could be at the center folded up, disappeared
A fine red mist

I think before I wake up, before
I am all the way awake, that tonight will be
the night before when everything is on the eve of happening

I can sleep, it is the night before, the day before
I can make it always be the day before
if I don't wake up

The Mess of Thrown Off Clothes

Strider Marcus Jones

i listen
to your love beads glisten
in the flotsam
of my room-

we make them
from samurai sword folds
at forge and loom
in the mess of thrown off clothes.

so many smoke me kisses
at portal doors,
and mithril wishes
on primitive floors-

take us back again
through heath and fen
to imitate
lost landscape-

cycle
and circle
sky and stone
outside and home-

in love in less
with your heavenliness,
and loneliness
durable under duress.

Solitary

Rick Doyle

I am a man
I am a man reading

a story in a newspaper
about another man

who languishes
in solitary confinement

whose age is that
of my own son.

Irish Hermitage Dream

Eileen 'ike' West

An invisible menace threatens.
I might blame the economy,
I could say it's people's indifference,
But it's not.
It is fear of the unknown, for sure.
An unlikely unknown;
As if lately, we're overshadowed by ghosts,
Phantoms from some dank corner of the collective mind.

Where once the group psyche held a semblance of
Peace and grace,
Darkness chokes out the light.
Marching heavy-footed into consciousness,
Innocent women deemed 'spoils' are cast down and raped.
Suspicious-looking individuals tortured for confessions,
Fodder for fashionable 'humane cruelty.'
Young soldiers bludgeoned,
Mired in their own bloody sludge.

From a hermit's cell in Ireland,
The long-dead Saint Kevin warns,
"Knocking such pesky visions from awareness,
Hain't yet thinkable.
Same as fleas on a dog,
Can chase the devils away, for one moment
Only to have 'em reappear in the next—
'Tis nothin' to do,
Lest like me, ye become reclusive."
From New York Harbor,
Lady Liberty's voice booms in retort,
"Try this—
Torch with my blaze, those marauding specters."
Elbow bent, she takes aim,

Shooting rays of red, green, and gold.
The Lady hits her mark, shrugs, and sighs,
"Alas, now we're naught, but witless."

Except to become hermits or feign rash ignorance,
There is no regenerating forsaken peace and grace,
No coming home to some idyllic state.
In today's war, does not matter where the battlefield,
The death toll rings,
Broadcast through every plane of sensibility,
Making sure the piper is paid in full.
And 'tis little to do for this blight on conscience, but suffer.

Time to recognize:
Warring itself must be conquered,
Every battle rounded up and scrutinized,
Like suspicious individuals
Sent to chambers for questioning,
Modern combat viewed as true 'spoils'
Must be thrown from patriotic pedestals,
Liberating minds bound exhaustively, in wars' bloody sludge.

Meanwhile, an invisible menace threatens.
I might blame the economy,
I could say it's people's indifference,
But it's not.
It is fear of the unknown, for sure.
But an unlikely unknown;
Overshadowed by ghosts,
Phantoms from our collective mind.

Bruised Orange

Patrick Dunn

Imagine waking every day in opulence
Seeing only ungilded spaces in need of gaudy excess
A photonegative emptiness
Too cracked to develop
Not even as interesting as the old canister of film
Mother left behind in the refrigerator
Back when child-mind wanted for cheap candy
And connection

What else went undeveloped?

Imagine staring,
Fixing something of thinning hair
In an ugly priceless mirror
Not noticing the reflection
Of the tower window
Sealed by fear some lifetime ago
Old man, no one
Is climbing the walls

A fear of fear!

Imagine, several times each day,
Eating what others have tested for poison
Others whose jobs you may have already cut
It's no accident that you feel the heartburn of power
The intense blood pressure
Grasping tightly to the
Sycophantic cyanide pill of a country
In decline

Imagine—

Doing it all the same tomorrow and tomorrow
And tomorrow still
Until death comes
With no repentance, no remorse
No other understanding
No understanding another
No peace but for the grace of your departure
And celebration in your wake

brick by brick

Melissa Lemay

the school was built
we sat in classrooms
each day, rote

memorization
of facts and figures
but never learning

about interest rates
or mortgages,
real-world, real-life

things we would use
(not) taught to think
in dewey decimal

systematically
ingrained with fracture
and parliament

defined by etiquette
and social order

i took out my retainer
and placed it on
my lunch tray,

and threw it in the trash
i understood quickly
that a new retainer

cost $200 and was
told not to do that again
i did it once more

My Body, Your Choice
Skylar Clark

Written November 8, 2024 at 1:00am—an hour after the election results.

I always dreamed of having children.
Two boys. Two girls.
That dream, that vision,
it's been with me as long as I can remember.
A life of love & chaos,
laughter echoing through the halls
of a big house on open land.
Dogs running wild, playing with the kids.
Their only worry?
What's for dinner?
Which movie will we watch tonight?

I dreamed of a future where love was enough,
where life unfolded as it should,
and where I got to decide what happened next.
Funny how life works out.

A little about me:

In 2002, I was born in Texas—
a place where a woman's body
has never been hers.
And my childhood was stolen,
abused by the very people
who were supposed to protect me.
The first time I learned
I was nothing but an object.

In 2006, I was adopted,
saved from the nightmare,
finally safe in my own skin.

In 2022, Roe v. Wade was overturned—
My choice was now
a memory.

A basic right—
—stripped away.
My body, no longer mine.
A feeling I am all too familiar with.

So in 2022, I dared to ask—
Can I have children?
Something I wanted more than anything.
And in 2022, I learned—
If I ever got pregnant,
the baby might not survive.

And if it didn't,
the doctors can do nothing
but watch me bleed
and pray I make it out alive.

In 2024, a 23-count felon
runs against a former Attorney General
for president.
It sounds like the start of a joke, right?
But no—this is the hell we're living in.

74 million Americans voted him in—
and their message?
Clear.
Loud.
You don't matter.
Your body is nothing.
It's a tool, a machine.
Something to use, something to discard.

In 2024, I grieve.

Grieve the home I'll never own.
The children I'll never bear.
The life I dreamed of,
ripped from me,
before I even had a chance.

In 2024, my dreams were crushed underfoot,
shattered,
trampled into the dirt.
I am nothing but property to you—
Just another thing to control,
To take,
To use,
Until there's nothing left.

This isn't just about those who
don't want children.
This is about the countless women
whose lives will be stolen,
whose futures will be erased—
because of the choices you made.
Because of your votes.
Your hatred.
Your control.
You. Chose. This.
You chose to take our rights.
You chose to silence our voices.
You chose to let men—
—men
decide what happens to our bodies.

You voted for this cruelty.
For the suffering.
For the deaths of women
who will never get the choice *you* took from them.
You wanted this.
You chose this.

And now you can't hide.

Don't look away from the blood *you* spilled.
Don't pretend *you* didn't choose
to let women die.

Because *you* did.
***You*. Chose. This.**

You don't get to wash your hands clean.
You don't get to ignore the screams,

the pain,
the death.

You decided we were nothing.
You decided our bodies were your choice—
and now,
you will live with that decision.
You will carry the weight of every life lost,
every woman who dies,
every future that ends,
because of the vote ***you*** cast.

We will never forgive.
And we will never forget
the blood
that is on ***your*** hands.

Hope

Rachel Armes-McLaughlin

Days like today
it feels like all's about to end.

The earthquakes with thousands lost.
The floods, never seen before.
The fires consume forest and home.

Democracy gone.

Then nights like tonight, there's hope restored:

Cory Booker on the senate floor,
making history. A record broke.
Wisconsin, fighting back against purchased votes.

Blue Violets at the park,
and news of a new, unexpected home.

The battle, uphill–but hope.

Hope.

Vanishing Into…

Kate Bremer

Luminous darkness between rooster calls
Looking into pupil-less goat
eyes, connecting with her nose, the quiver,
the crevice, the device, crevasse, the divine,
Divide. Birdsong. The pottery next door--
Cracked and kilned and built. Stop
And hear the aftermath of death--
Crater of belonging--clotheslines full,
Toys hidden, casinos buzzing. Far away
Donkey speaks, not one of ours.
Forest Service mules have been fired;
Some don't care about livestock auctions,
Trucks to Mexico, medicines for children,
School lunch or family separation.
River rock is a theme today--
Lay in the sun in the layer of the lairs of water.

Everyone Loses in this Monopoly Game

Merril D. Smith

The first square is empty, walk
on the beach, envision a city,
build it, they will come,

ferry to railroad, Philadelphia day-trippers,
vacationers, escapers, walk the Boardwalk,
it's the place to be seen—

women in diamonds and furs—turn a corner, jump
a square, find the bootleggers and bookies,
make a deal,
over there, a new hotel.

On another square, see my grandfather
in a black and white photo swagger
across the boards, hat atop his head,
his gambling connections seem almost quaint.

Continue your ramble round the squares,
my parents honeymoon while soldiers train
and find romance in WWII.

Move on—more squares hold
the Miss America pageant and union conventions,
Frank Sinatra, a diving horse at Steel Pier,

the city rises and falls, houses are torn down
to construct casinos, the gaudiest of all,
a façade fixtured with fool's gold,

so many squares are filled by cons, not pros,
corruption greases the game with slime
the slimiest robber-baron,

would be a red-capped king,
line-up to roll the dice
take a chance you will be paid—
but now

he locks the Community Chest, carries it
to Florida, he is the monopoly,
he grasps the Stay Out of Jail card,
waves it like a flag.

Maverick

Adam G. House

The emperor has no clothes,
throwing rocks from his glass house,
atop his ivory towers,
watching each quiet church mouse.

Oppressing the subjects with his greedy dictates—
self-serving proclamations for power.
Thieving sleight of hand from behind his holy veil:
sanctimonious stench, sheep-skinned wolf, thorny fading flower.

The royal lighthouse goes dim,
but the patriarch says it's getting brighter.
The masses blindly surrender faith to his word,
and his comforting grip grows ever tighter.

Paper monarchs presiding over a house of cards,
building little kingdoms around big egos,
perpetrating ignorance with their scholarly wisdom,
drunk on power unchecked by any veto.

One voice cries out:
"All is not as it should be,
all is not as it seems.
Man is meant to live free!"

Who is this lowly peon
daring to question the kingdoms?
Such independence isn't acceptable—
these foolish notions of individual freedoms.

Ordained of God and for the greater good,
we stand on what is absolutely right.
There is no room for heretics and dissent,
irreverent to trust in one's own guiding light.

The authorities in power may not be questioned.
You must dispense with speaking as you feel.
Suppress that rebellious spirit.
We shall teach you what is real.

But the lonely voice exclaims again:
"I must satisfy my own mind.
The integrity of truth is my highest calling—
and this is what I must find."

But the aristocracy casts out the traitor,
damned his darkness and confusion.
We shall bear witness to the judgment for his candor,
holding to our grandiose illusions.

The eccentric heretic wanders away
from the tall cities of pure light,
down a lonely, deserted path
into the eerily irresistible night.

It is here the outcast sees a truth
the city of lights hid in its splendor.
The inquisitive mind is drawn to the dark,
where curiosity may yield hidden treasures.

You see, when the lights are so bright
and all the answers come too easy,
where the city walls keep out the dark and taboo,
and all the king's robots bid to his pleasing...

The darkness without is shrouded in mystery and fear,
as discouragement and coercion
drive ponderings from the mind.
The rest of life's experiences remain undiscovered—
unless you're a maverick,
willing to face what you may find.

when asked for help writing a satire

Matthew E. Henry

she said it was due in a few hours. so I closed my laptop,
stopped grading, and did my colleague's job. taught her
the classic definitions and offered some examples. but
she was too Black to watch *SNL* and too young to remember
In Living Color. so I re-opened my laptop and showed her
a *Key & Peele* sketch—how, in a post-apocalyptic suburb,
"some racist motherfucking zombies" slouch and skulk
away from an easy meal of dark meat. how their ragged,
outstretched arms recoil from terrified, then confused
Black bodies searching for safety once Kevin Sorbo
was consumed. brain-frenzied chads locking car doors
with broken windows. undead karens clutching drooling
daughters like purses from brains they fear are filled
with crack rock, fried chicken, and cop-killing gangsta rap
all because they're "some racist motherfucking zombies."

it clicked. she vigorously nodded then explained her drafted idea:
a orange-leaved tree running for president of *Forestlandia*
so he could clear the woods of the groves he despised.
it's February of 2025: a little on the nose, but she understood
the assignment. still, I told her she wasn't going far enough.
that to be truly satirical she needed something more. like
the fuckary of the trees voting against their own self-interest.
maybe offering more room for their saplings if lumber is sold
to the local mill, but somehow they never believe the hacksaw
will ever hew and fell them. I admit I got too excited crafting
possibilities. at rallies, trees chanting *BURN AND CLEAR!*
and *CUT US DOWN!* Spanish Oaks being used to build a wall
around *Forestlandia,* the Ebony for bonfires and crosses.

she gave me a sad look as she began to pack her things.
she thanked me for the help, patted me on the shoulder.

Inauguration
Bartholomew Barker

The Emperor strode across the stage, declaring
he'd woven his suit and robes from the purest gold
and they were the classiest, comfortablest clothes
he or anyone had ever worn.

Social media saluted, his cultists cheered,
grateful reporters transcribed every word,
and very serious pundits on television debated
both sides of his glory.

But the poets and children pointed and laughed
at his flabby delusions and flaccid dingle.

Elon, Jeff and Mark asserted
no one could possibly see
through his magnificent new clothes
and that it was clearly huge.

All the Naked Emperors

Patricia J McLean

If we put them end to end all the naked men
all the naked emperors from the first
in earth's history to the last
they would circle the globe.
A million moons shining up at the sky
their mouths full of dirt
their penises sticking into the soft earth
and their anuses would be singing
reaching for a high note
describing their glorious raiment
their illustrious careers
how the people loved them and how
they changed the world.

The Spark

R.M. Carlson

a heart breaks again,
and another,
and another…

each time, each tear
each betrayal
devastation
the thread of love
follows
the sharp needle:

binding, mending, strengthening
love awakening, eyes opening
to the collective consciousness

love abides in all
a light to shine
the spark must be struck
by the needle:

binding, mending, strengthening
weaving all together
as one

stronger together
one love, one light
darkness is only
where light
has not yet
been brought

The Silent Era

Rick Doyle

There was a time when Max was silent as a moon,
as a satellite in transit behind the lunar pebble,
as a man whose mouth is shoveled full of earth.

It wasn't just that he couldn't speak
in public -- oh, no! He couldn't whisper
sweet nothings, couldn't utter a prayer,
couldn't even tell a knock-knock joke.
And this had come on him all at once.
He was twenty-one years old, he'd just
graduated from college, where incidentally
he'd never lacked the confidence to speak,
asking questions in the lecture hall,
answering them, too, not shrinking even
from arguing with his instructors.
Sharing observations. My God,
in those days, dripping with faith
in his own, as it turns out, quite orthodox beliefs,
Max yearned to be a professor!
It wasn't until after he'd earned his bachelor's
that he found himself utterly bereft of the gift
of speech, no more capable of opening his mouth
and holding forth than Demosthenes
before the saving lozenge, than Isaiah before
the burning coal touched his prophetic lips.

But for Max there was no burning coal.
No one, least of all Max, knows what it was
that delivered him from what could have been,
for all practical purposes,
the life of a desert father,
making possible a law school career
wherein he withstood for three years, albeit without

distinction, the withering fire of the Socratic method.
The cure remains as mysterious
as the source of his affliction,
but look at him now: here's Max, rising from where
he sits, at the table of the accused, standing and turning
toward the bench, opening his mouth to speak,
launching into another of his closing arguments:

Your Honor, with all due respect to my learned brother,
on this record the state has failed to meet its burden...

Ego Death

Aubrey Phoenix

That's what I mean, though-
Everything has burned down.
I'm rising from the ashes,
Albeit traumatized and shaken,
But I've never felt more alive.
It feels like The Universe
Has stripped me down to my bare soul-
Pulled me apart into pure essence,
Leaving behind scattered nouns and adjectives
That I've claimed in this life,
Ultimately, it all means nothing.

I mean, seriously;
I was once a daughter,
Now I want to be a son.
Instead, I'm not sure I exist at all.
Certainly not to my parents.

So, which is true?
I used to be Savanna
But I don't even know who that is anymore
I was her once, but she is not me now.

How could one's ego *not* die in these conditions?

Nothing tangible lasts,
You can acquire things, but what's the point
When one day the other shoe will drop
And you'll lose it all anyway?

Staring down the cliff, I inevitably have to dive,
About to lose my pets, my bed, and my mind.
It's terrible, but I can't help but laugh maniacally,

And not just because I'm off my meds.
Raw truth is often found in insanity,
Though most fear unfiltered notions-
They don't want candor unless it's sparkly.

I mean, this is just *"another one of those"* situations to me.
I feel like I'm ultimately doomed to die and lose it all,
But somehow, I survive the blaze every time.

Believe me, I'm not cocky.
I know it's a dangerous line to walk
And that each day that I breathe fresh air
Is a gift for which I am very grateful.

The Mad Hatter Hiding in Dark Matter

Strider Marcus Jones

in our house
i binned the radio
for playing Strauss-

left the suited rodeo
of casino Faust
and shot the gentry shooting grouse.

into the wild garden
without spun jargon
we went

through rusting arch of rose dissent
onto the precipice of peace
where slush borders grip and grease

like usurping tectonic plates
shapeshifting smaller states.
their innocents bombed and dispossessed

join our shoaled oppressed
of obedient possessed-
while The Mad Hatter

hiding in Dark Matter-
says blame them, instead of Strauss
in suits playing casino Faust

and enslaving gentry shooting grouse.

You prefer

Rick Doyle

horseradish to mustard
turnip to maple syrup

Dutchman's breeches to hawkweed
a ditch full of asters to a field of daisies

head of tide to estuary
tomorrow's eclipse to last year's comet

a broken promise to a broken-backed threat
a heartfelt obscenity to a misleading song
a bitter truth to a brass-belled anthem

a feathered doubt to a copper certainty
a zealous uncertainty to a willful faith
a shattered faith to a chrome-plated doubt.

Ubuntu

Andrew Frewin Wilson

When our humanity falters
In so many places
And what really matters
Is trounced in so many ways
When dictators are not just
A "Third" World affliction
Which "First" encouraged, in moral dereliction
And now is itself spotted like rust
With rampant would-be elite Fascism
We can draw back from the abyss
For democracy is no mere -ism
If "humanity" no longer resonates, then think on this
There are other words from other places you
Can use so why not try "Ubuntu"?

Ubuntu *is not just a philosophical concept but a way of life that influences social interactions, justice, and community building. It reminds us of our shared humanity and the importance of supporting one another.*

No Eulogy

Chad Parenteau

Priest reads
cliff notes,
from obit.

Lived, worked,
retired, died,
had family.

What else
gets buried
this afternoon?

Not a single
secret passed
over pew.

Soon no one
will recall
anyone here.

Final gift
of holy
anonymity.

Just one
more thread
on bootstrap.

The unsung
of world's
winning team.

Sweeping

themselves
under rug.

Pass Peter
without ever
showing pass.

Behind gates,
faceless divine
forevermore.

Consequences

Benjamin Waldrum

They'll come for you next, you can count on that fact;
They'll keep coming so long as there's more to subtract.
They'll trumpet their values — no faults, only gloss;
They'll arrive wrapped in the flag and carrying a cross.

They'll reduce human rights with the stroke of a pen;
They'll betray their own people, then betray them again.
They'll brag the economy (read: profits) is at record highs;
They'll not care there are few to whom that applies.

They'll add more undesirables to their growing list;
They'll enforce your birth gender and decide who you'll kiss.
They'll white out their own failures and replace them with wins;
They'll misinform and control, making resistance appear thin.

They'll restrict options to choose, but that's only begun;
They'll want to lower your free choice to just one.
They'll declare that your principles and beliefs are untrue;
They'll lament that you don't understand like they do.

They'll tell you this is all for the good of the cause;
They'll ignore or remove any troublesome laws.
They'll chip away at the wonderful things you hold dear;
They'll point out that you voted — was this result not unclear?

They'll make truths from their lies and clothe it in hate; and
They'll say all of these things make America great.

The Samaritan Machine

Strider Marcus Jones

this field pond
is only my
dissolved
imagination-
thought drops
of summer rain
making fractal ripples
drumbeat on skin.
a portal shared
with cawing crows
reveals
who scams and snoops and shoots
in contract conversations.
this Windsong
of Virginia Creeper,
ruling Bear and Wolfsbane
rustling in black bamboo
trusts its Samaritan Machine
telling it who to redact
in this imposed
dystopian
equilibrium
of dumbed-down masses
worshipping Carousel.

Sexes

Aubrey Phoenix

I didn't like myself
When I was acceptable to others.

My family would tell you
That I was most successful
When I worked for Sexes-
A seemingly stable 9-6,
Hardly above poverty pay
Relative to the tech-forward
Norcal SF Peninsula…
But it came with an apartment,
Health insurance, for the first time in my adult life,
And a little bit of walking around money-
Sure, I can see how it would all seem ideal
From the lens of a society built on accepting
The absolute bare minimum…

That is, until anything went awry,

Then it all went to the vet,
To the doctor,
To my car,
To the government.

I ran that hamster wheel because
It didn't look like one
Until you get inside.
I put on the business casual monkey suit,
Adhered to all the corporate rules
That meant I was no longer
An individual.
Not at work.
Not in my employee housing.

Not even in therapy;
Hidden in the fine print,
Sexes could ask for any/all of my secrets.
I desperately tried to hold it all together
The façade, the pleasant face,
And the tone of voice to keep customers,
Management,
Friends and family all at ease.
Everyone, but me.
Only at the end of the day
While I stared into the void
Of my ever-growing list of tasks
I was too drained to complete-
Only then could my brow crease
And my mind spin-
I was no longer human,
But a confused animal,
Chained to the confines of my cage,
Groomed to fit the image
Of the corporate zoo.

My mind and body fought continuously,
Spilling out of the mold that wasn't made to fit me-
As a born woman,
Nonbinary by design;
As a bipolar autistic with PTSD,
Too spicy to be typical.
Eventually, my body rejected everything I put into it.
Caffeine and cannabis were the compulsory cocktail
That kept me from total collapse
Until it didn't.

Something in me, all the while
Refused to be tamed
My differentness, my voice.
They tried to silence it,
But I never could.

Instead, it brewed within me
Demanding to be seen, heard, expressed-
Until it was so loud it screamed, sobbed, and pleaded
To be let out.
Stridence deafened everything else
Until my delicate, glass life
Shattered around me
And left me sprawled in the wreckage
With pieces too small to reassemble.

So, rather than try in vain to refashion the frame
I made myself into a rather queer mosaic.

Tinder

Andrew Frewin Wilson

"It needn't be tinder, this juncture of the year"
—*Conor O'Callaghan, January Drought*

I – Hand-wringing…

Tinseltown they called it
The Hollywood sign above it
On mountain and canyons covered
With scrub like gasoline tinder
Rich palaces of dreams rendered
To which many young locusts aspired
But Santa Anna winds have burned
Those houses to naught but ash
Chimneys only gravestones to the cash
Will Angelinos now have learned
Money, for Nature is no match
Challenge it and there's a catch
Will L.A. be a lesson to us all
That Damocles' sword's about to fall…

II – Thunderbolt slinging…

"Come friendly bombs and rain on Slough"
Quipped English Poet Laureate
Enough with all this rational debate
No one heeds "We the People" now
Let Mar-a-Lago flooded be
With Trump inside preferably
Let insurance baulk at rebuilding
The Palace-ades of rich and famous
And let's see what Trump really does
When Global Warming's truly a thing
So unlike wise old King Canute
The science is no longer moot
And yes, for sure we all will suffer
Till Nature trumps the monstrous duffer…

Indigenous People's Night

Chad Parenteau

Auto shop stays open
to grill burgers among
the unfinished labor.

Radio on Latin beats
hope's fast drums speed
passersby away quickly.

All feel indigenous
somewhere. Anyone
could be a colonist

who wants to settle
both feet on our backs
like branding irons.

Above, moon seeks
asylum in clouds, fears
being discovered again.

say what you mean

another nonet

Matthew E. Henry

an affirmative action hire
a multicultural hire
a diversity hire
an equity hire
a DEI... just
be honest and
call me *a*
nigger,
please.

Echoes

Patricia J McLean

I'm at the edge of a cliff looking over,
looking over at the cracks in the rock on
the other side. I'm at the cliff edge
where time stretches, arcs back-forward,
ages stacked on ages bent, arched,
tilted, earth colors, life, death, beginning, end.

I'm at the edge of the cliff. I imagine I can see
the other side. I'm on the edge of the cliff,
I can't see the bottom. Gravel grinds in my knees.
You didn't think I was standing? I wouldn't stand
at the edge of a crumbling cliff. Every minute
something falls in it. The rim crumbles in my fingers.
I'm on the edge and my voice, my cries, echo

on the canyon walls. I had no Idea I was so loud, so terrified,
so calm. My whispers can still be heard. People turn to look at me.
I'm not alone. You didn't think I was alone at the edge of the cliff?
We're all here at the edge. Some people lie on their backs looking up.
Others stand as if that weren't dangerous, they
look back the way we've come, maybe they are thinking
about going home. Everyone is here.

Sand in my mouth, my teeth hiss. I slide forward.
I can see the bottom of the canyon, the river that would
take me away if I fell over the edge. I'm on my belly. You didn't think
I was on my knees? No it's worse than that. So much worse.
I am here with billions of people and I am on my belly, clinging
to the last bit of earth at the edge of the cliff.
Far below, the river is dry.

Untitled

Kate Bremer

1. Medicare Test (from Naomi Shihab Nye)

What year is it? Sunday?
What's the donkey's name;
Why is she wearing orange slippers?
Draw a Kit Kat Klock--her Krazy eyes
And rigid plastic tail are mine.

Drinking water, Meals on Wheels;
I won't write about killing children
(or adults) in Gaza
Ukraine, Salvador. First
They took the Venezuelans.
Can you pass a Medicare test
If you are steeped in conspiracy--
A member of the death cult?

All I know is Blue Bees
Live on my porch.

2. Antreena

Wind is here and birdsong,
John Prine and Townes--
Burnt out fires warm the cabin walls.
Keep breathing. Squirrels on the roof,
Keep the compost tuning,
Read a poem a day and wear a winter hat
In April. Carolina Wren. Wend.
Scrambling the signal. My antenna today
Is this ancient oak, Arabella.
No crypto, no AI, no A1, just branches
And leaves. I swear my clock has stopped;

Spider webs catch debris, decorate the tear,
tier, tree. Tree tears are bending time
Bigfoot cloaks in the bark, Barks in the cloak
Old glass wind chime, bones toweled
Into rock walls, limbs make
Window screens. Screams.

3. Big Hands

Bad weedeater, bats,
Bad chainsaw, bad bullets.
Let the kittens drink, feed
The Odalisque. Let her rest…
I love a cantina with colored
Light bulbs and Aztec calendars.

Crunching donkeys, hawk and titmouse.
Hay presence, tangled mane, frogs
Touch ground and sing at night;
Fox calls screech owl. Tiny wires
And flashes in my brain spark heart
And hands and purple ink.

My calendar is pre-Equinox,
Pre-birdsong, *Kwanza begins*
And Boxing Day--writing on
December. Donkey reaches quietude.
Stillness and Community--
Birdsong and Blue Bees will bring us home.

What We Tend

Meridith Allison

The long and short of it is,
I'd rather not be listening to a podcast
about how democracies die
as I pull weeds on a Saturday morning
while the American flag on my neighbor's porch
flaps loudly in the wind.

But this much I know: summer remembers both the gardener
and the absence of one.

The long and short of it is,
I have two sons, not yet caught up in the life ahead of them,
their days filled with Minecraft and marble runs,
chess openings and lightsaber duels.

But of this I'm sure: the empire of childhood, like all empires,
falls slowly at first, and then all at once.

And so I teach my gentle boys
of Napoleon III and the Reichstag fire,
Kent State, Selma, Tiananmen Square,
the rise of Mussolini and the fall of Rome.
We learn *Habeas corpus, coup d'état, la migra!, la migra!, et tu, Brute?*

And I ask them to notice
the bowl in the sink before the oatmeal hardens,
the sock on the floor, passed over for days,
the sirens, the scared, the hungry, the helpers.
Where do the lizards get their water?

The long and short of it is,
I'm still trying to figure this out for myself.
Do we fight fire with fire?

Look for the cracks, push where it leans?
Do we run, do we wait, do we garden, can we grieve?

I think:
you can only fight a tyrant where your feet touch the ground.

I think:
the roots that we tend will return in the spring.

Keep Going

Rachel Armes-McLaughlin

Small twigs on the pavement
look like so many tiny bones—
phalanges and miniature fibulae.

Underfoot, they roll, still fresh
enough that they do not crack.
There is a me-sized bowl in the

earth ahead near the creek—
a womb-like hollow that I
desperately long to crawl inside.

I keep going, keenly aware that
so many others walk with me
in collective grief, even if not here.

The old baseball field is nearly empty,
a lone crow yelling at vacant stands,
or maybe ghosts of those long gone.

The few leaves remaining shake
on limbs like pom-poms across
the track, sounding like distant applause,

the sentiment: "You're almost there!"
Are we almost there? I am so tired.
Even so, it is a bright, crisp morning.

Birds sing. Leaves drift beautifully.
Are we almost there? I don't think so.
But walk with me—

Even if you are not here.

Learning about Nazis in High School

Bartholomew Barker

Reading my history texts, I imagined
what I would've done if I'd lived
in Germany during the War.

How I would've resisted, hidden Jews
in my basement, risked my life,
my freedom to foil the fascists.

But having grown-up and fat,
I sign petitions, write letters
to the editor and merely vote.

I don't think I could fit a secret
room behind my poetry bookshelf,
much less an underground railroad.

I used to wonder how the Good Germans
could have been so blind?

Now I know and I am shamed.

Emerging from the Penumbra

Merril D. Smith

In scant light, slant light, shadows stroll
above the bones unseen,
remains of scattered, shattered lives,
Glory, Hallelujah, we used to sing.

Was this then, or is this now?
The truth is marching on--
torn, twisted, and trampled
in scant, slant light as shadows stroll,

as masked men menace, muscled marauders
from obscurity troll

in the scant, slant light of spring,
the grass is greening, the days are growing,
the roses blooming,

the shattered bones are speaking,

calling not for "bombs bursting in air,"
but my country, "sweet land of liberty,"
always a vision, yet there it is—listen—

the susurrus of ghost voices
songs from the shadows lift
"we shall overcome,"
march on, march on, march on, march on.

*"But when Newton's apple fell toward the earth,
the earth, ever so slightly, fell toward the apple as well."*

— Ellen Bass, *The World Has Need of You*

Contributor Bios

Meridith Allison lives on the edge of the Gila Wilderness in southwestern New Mexico with her family. She writes often, finishes pieces occasionally, and shares her work rarely-usually only when her brother, who happens to be the editor of this project, insists. She's very fond of walking and of her little dog, Boo.

Rachel Armes-McLaughlin has written poetry for nearly 25 years. Her work is published in *Loblolly Press; Middle Mouse Press; Medicine and Meaning*, where she has reviewed poetry; and a Central Arkansas Library System anthology, with one poem nominated for Best of the Net. Rachel lives in the very red state of Arkansas with her husband, Jack; daughter, Isabelle; and cats, Wednesday and Mera. She attended her first protest in early 2025 and is looking forward to soon attending another.

Bartholomew Barker works with Living Poetry. He has published a full-length collection, a chapbook, and been nominated for a Pushcart and the Best of the Net. His work has recently appeared in *Autumn Sky Poetry Daily, Panoply, Tipton Poetry Journal, Gyroscope Review* and the *Naugatuck River Review* among others. www.bartbarkerpoet.com

Kate Bremer lives in Central Texas and loves to host writing gatherings in nature with her small herd of donkeys and a horse.

With a B.S. in Communications, **R.M. Carlson**'s career over the years covered marketing, public relations, and scientific and research journal management and publishing. As a child, she wrote and illustrated stories and has continued to write as a hobby ever since. Her focus shifted to poetry after taking a college poetry class. Her strong sense of social justice was established early in life by the ideals of her working class parents, who actively engaged in politics, community, and more. She was raised in a church with progressive values that actively fought for social justice in and outside the local area. R.M. Carlson now seeks ways she can make a difference, however small, in the world. Poetry has become her middle finger extended toward fascism.

Chris Chan is an educator and amateur poet based in New Jersey. He works as an administrator for the Department of English at the University of Pennsylvania, where he earned his Ph.D. He has published research articles on poetry, politics, and the history of literary criticism in *Eighteenth-Century Studies* and *Eighteenth-Century Life*. You can find his poems and other personal writings on his WordPress blog, "The Phoenix Tree Writes," at: reentry8.wordpress.com.

Skylar Clark is a 23-year-old writer and animal welfare advocate from East Texas. A survivor and storyteller, she uses her voice to illuminate the intersections of personal trauma and political injustice. Skylar works in animal rescue and is a passionate activist for stronger animal protection laws across the South, often saying she's "a voice for the voiceless"—both human and animal. Her writing is intimate, urgent, and unafraid, rooted in lived experience and the fight for autonomy, safety, and change.

Rick Doyle, poet and playwright, practices law in Downeast Maine. His poetry has been published in numerous journals, including *Kaleidotrope* and *The Cafe Review*, and won a SpiritWord Honors Award from the Maine Poetries Collective. His one-act play, *Regalia*, was selected as a winner in the Maine Playwrights Contest and presented in readings at Acorn School of Performing Arts, Stonington Opera House, and elsewhere. He has recently completed *Regina Snowdeal*, a full-length play exploring the efforts of a survivor of domestic violence to reunite with her son after he has been removed from her home by the state.

Patrick Dunn is a writer and musician living in Sacramento, CA. He earned his MFA from Stony Brook University and has published pieces in various journals. In addition to writing, he is the executive director of a nonprofit that supports patients with rare autoimmune diseases.

Bonner Fowles is an Austin-born artist based in Central Texas. His acrylic-on-canvas painting *June14th* was created on that very day in response to the protests and events happening then, and serves as the cover artwork for this collection.

Shannon Frost Greenstein (She/They) resides near Philadelphia with her family and cats. She is the author of *Through the Lens of Time* (2026), a forthcoming fiction collection with Thirty West Publishing, and *These Are a Few of My Least Favorite Things* (2022), a book of poetry from Really Serious Lit. Shannon is a former Ph.D. candidate in Continental Philosophy and a multi-time Pushcart Prize nominee. Her work has appeared in *McSweeney's Internet Tendency*, *Pithead Chapel*, *Bending Genres*, *SoFloPoJo*, and elsewhere. Shannon's passions include Friedrich Nietzsche, anti-racism, the Seven Summits, the *Hamilton* soundtrack, motherhood, and acquiring more cats. Find her at shannonfrostgreenstein.com or on Twitter and Bluesky at @shannonfrostgre. Insta: @zarathustra_speaks

Matthew E. Henry (MEH) is the author of six poetry collections, most recently *said the Frog to the scorpion* (Harbor Editions, 2024). He is editor-in-chief of *The Weight Journal*, the creative nonfiction editor at *Porcupine Literary*, and an associate editor at *Rise Up Review*. MEH's publications include *Barren Magazine*, *Anti-Heroin Chic*, *Had*, *Massachusetts Review*, *Mayday*, *Mom Egg Review*, *Ploughshares*, *Redivider*, *Stone Circle Review*, *Terrain*, *Whale Road Review*, and *The Worcester Review*. MEH is a high school teacher who received his MFA yet continued to spend money he didn't have completing an MA in theology, and a PhD in education. He writes about education, race, religion, and burning oppressive systems to the ground at MEHPoeting.com.

Adam G. House is known by some as a licensed Muay Thai Kru/coach/teacher/instructor (Muay Thai International Association, Bangkok), retired United States Army Airborne combat veteran, retired drummer, writer/author, liber(al)tarian independent, eXvangelical (former licensed minister), atheistic-Satanist (secular skeptic, agnostic anti-theist), and perpetual autodidact who is currently pursuing college degrees in law and the social sciences as a non-traditional (old) student. However, Kru Adam likes to think of himself as a sovereign sentient mortal of no particular significance. substack.com/@independentthinker/posts

Strider Marcus Jones is a poet, law graduate, and former civil servant from Salford, England with proud Celtic roots in Ireland and Wales. He is the editor and publisher of *Lothlorien Poetry Journal* (lothlorienpoetryjournal.blogspot.com). A member of The Poetry Society, nominated for the Pushcart Prize x3 and Best of the Net x3, his five published books of poetry (stridermarcusjonespoetry.wordpress.com) reveal a maverick, moving between cities, playing his saxophone in smoky rooms. His poetry has been published in numerous publications including *Poppy Road Review*, *The Galway Review*, *The Huffington Post USA*, *The Stray Branch Literary Magazine*, *Crack The Spine Literary Magazine*, *The Lampeter Review*, *Panoplyzine Poetry Magazine*, and *Dissident Voice*.

Melissa Lemay lives in Lancaster County, Pennsylvania, with her children, cats, and dog. She writes about God, addiction, trauma, healing, motherhood, and many other things. She enjoys spending time with family, drinking good coffee, and being outdoors. She loves animals. Her poem, *Ephemeral*, was chosen as Poetic Publication of the Year for 2023 at *Spillwords Press*; she was Author of the Month for July 2024 and Author of the Year for 2024. Find her at melissalemay.wordpress.com, collaborature.blogspot.com, and at *dVerse Poets Pub*.

Liz Mariani's work has been published in *Two Serious Ladies*, *Italian Trans Geographies* (edited by Danila Cannamela, Marzia Mauriello, and Summer Minerva via SUNY Press), *Great Lakes Review*, *The Waiting Room*, *The Buffalo News*, *After The Pause*, and *Advaitam Speaks*. Find her at linktr.ee/lizmarianipoetry

Sue McBean is a nurse teacher, sailor, wildflower photographer, and botanist who writes creatively. Living many years now on the North coast of Northern Ireland, she was brought up on the flat lands of the Cambridgeshire Fens. Sue writes mainly prose with poetic style, reflecting on her life, exploring themes of sea, sailing, island life, and nature. She is interested in overlaying difficult experiences with beauty, art and laughter and is currently writing a memoir, a series of essays about well-being and children's stories.

Patricia J McLean lives in Bend, Oregon. Her work has appeared in various publications including *Windfall*, *The Lake*, *Panache*, and *Trillium*. She and her spouse, Duane Poncy, have collaborated on three novels, *Degrees of Freedom* (2025), *Ghosts of Saint-Pierre* (2022), and *Bartlett House* (2007), and are working on their fourth novel. They established Rainy Nights Press in 2003, editing and publishing *Raising Our Voices*, an honored anthology introduced by Ursula K. Le Guin and Judith Barrington. The press published *Navigation* by Brittney Corrigan, *Red Dust Rising* by Marilyn Johnston, *Like the Sun in Storm* by Ralph Salisbury, and *Eye of the Moon* by Australian author Shelly Davidow. Beginning in 2012, they published *Elohi Gadugi Journal*, an online magazine of poetry, short stories, and non-fiction. They co-hosted the popular poetry series *Readings at Milepost 5* (Portland, OR) for five years.
Patricia's website is poncy-mclean.net

Aubrey Phoenix is a twenty-six-year-old nonbinary, neurodivergent, alternative artist struggling to survive in America—but surely not the only one. Raised in a self-help, toxically positive "it's all in your head if you get sick" household, they hastened away from adolescence into adulthood, naively trusting that the world would welcome them on a path to their destined success. Their rose-tinted glasses shattered when their existence and truth proved time and time again to be something they would have to fight for. Their first book, *All The Things I Left Unfinished*, shares poems from some of their rawest moments of self-discovery—harrowing accounts of parental trauma, heartbreak, and struggles with bipolar II disorder in early adulthood. Five years, lots of lore, disowning, and some domestic violence later, they continue to scream out loud—still trying to make sense of their life and their place in a society that would prefer they stay quiet or cease to exist. Healing, growing, and humbling are lifelong quests—but Aubrey carries on sharing their story in hopes of reaching others who have been forsaken by a family and a world that they once hoped would make space for them, or at the very least let them be. You can find more of Aubrey's work on their new website, aubreyphoenix.com

Chad Parenteau hosts Boston's long-running Stone Soup Poetry series. His work has appeared in journals such as *Résonancee*, *Molecule*, *Ibbetson Street*, *Pocket Lint*, *Cape Cod Poetry Review*, *Tell-Tale Inklings*, *Off*

The Coast, The Crossroads, The Skinny Poetry Journal, The New Verse News, dadakuku, Nixes Mate Review, and *The Ugly Monster.* He has also been published in anthologies such as *French Connections, Sounds of Wind, Reimagine America,* and *The Vagabond Lunar Collection.* His newest collections are *All's Well Isn't You* and *Cant Republic: Erasures and Blackouts.* He serves as Associate Editor of the online journal *Oddball Magazine* and co-organizer of the annual Boston Poetry Marathon. He lives and works in Boston.

Phoebe Shade is a young artist based in Austin, Texas, who enjoys working in both digital and traditional media. Her first published works—a poem titled *Magic Doors* and an acrylic painting titled *Stargazing Cat on a Beach at Midnight*—appeared in *Poems for Tomorrow,* Issue 3. She enjoys creating art that blends imagination with real-life experiences.

Merril D. Smith is an independent scholar and Pushcart-nominated poet. She writes from southern New Jersey. Her work has been published widely in poetry journals and anthologies. Her full-length poetry collection, *River Ghosts* (Nightingale & Sparrow Press), was Black Bough Poetry's December 2022 Book of the Month. Find her at Bluesky: @merrildsmith.bsky.social; Instagram: mdsmithnj; Blog: merrildsmith.org

Benjamin Waldrum lives in Little Rock, Arkansas, where he writes for the health care sector. A former journalist and technical writer, he believes strongly in the malleability of language and the power of storytelling to inspire and effect change. His poetry has been published in the University of Arkansas for Medical Sciences' *Medicine & Meaning* literary journal.

Eileen 'ike' West, MA, is an international teacher and writer featured in Susan Smit's *Wise Women* (NL 2003) and Susan Taylor's *Sexual Radiance* (US 1998). Across decades, West's essays liberally sprinkle magazines and other publications in the US, UK, and EU. Samples are available at ikewest.com. West's first poetry collection, *Whistler of Petty Crimes*(2023), and earlier novels, *Away from Hannah's Castle* (US/NL 2006) and *Another Giant World* (UK 2018), are available through various and sundry outlets.

Andrew Frewin Wilson still works part-time as a factory manager in Bradford, West Yorkshire, and when not working, writes for pleasure. He has been a signwriter, painter, architectural draughtsman, as well as a restaurateur and held other food management roles. Working in many roles is a source of inspiration, and as an early adopter of reinvention every few years, his philosophy is: use it or lose it. Andrew is indebted to his AWA Writing Group and its facilitator, Deborah Bayer, for their nurturing and encouragement. how-would-you-know.com

Nick Allison is a former army infantryman, college dropout, and writer based in Austin, Texas. His work has appeared in *HuffPost*, *CounterPunch*, *The Shore*, *Eunoia Review*, *Kindred Characters Literary Journal*, *The Chaos Section*, and elsewhere. He served as editor for *Record of Dissent*. His poetry site is TheTruthAboutTigers.com. Also, he secretly enjoys writing his own bio in the third person because it probably makes him feel a little more important than he actually is.

Acknowledgments & Gratitude

First and foremost, this collection wouldn't exist without the generous spirit and conviction of the poets who trusted us with their work. At a time when speaking out carries real risk, each chose to lend their voice to a chorus of resistance. Through reflection, critique, and protest, your words give this project its power. Thank you for sharing them.

Several poems in this collection first appeared elsewhere:

"Irish Hermitage Dream" by Eileen 'ike' West was originally published in *Whistler of Petty Crimes* (Atmosphere Press, 2023).

"You Prefer" by Rick Doyle was first published online in *A Parallel Uni-verse*.

"Learning About Nazis in High School" by Bartholomew Barker originally published in *Dissident Voices*.

The quote from *How to Write One Song* by Jeff Tweedy appears in the epigraph courtesy of Dutton and Penguin Random House. We're grateful to Jeff and his team for their generous permission and encouragement—and to Wilco for providing the unofficial soundtrack to the editing process.

The quote from *The World Has Need of You* by Ellen Bass appears courtesy of Copper Canyon Press. Ellen, thank you for the poems that continue to offer clarity, compassion, and a deeper sense of what it means to stay present and awake in the world.

Special thanks to Bonner Fowles for creating the striking cover artwork—your vision brought everything together in a way that words alone couldn't.

To Phoebe Shade, for contributing the beautifully crafted interior illustration. It adds a quiet visual breath at the start of the book. Keep making art, Junebug. I love you.

To Melissa Lemay, who rescued me from the embarrassment of printing a couple of very obvious typos in the introduction— ones that somehow managed to sneak past me into the digital edition, despite being, well... very obvious.

To Meridith Allison, for being a final set of eyes before publication—your attention to detail and willingness to step in at the last moment helped make this stronger and more complete. One day, I hope to write with the same clarity and depth as my little sister. You really should share your poetry more often.

And to Rachel Armes-McLaughlin—your editorial feedback and careful reading made this collection sharper, more cohesive, and far more polished than it would have been otherwise. From one southern red-state dissenter to another, I hope we cross paths at a protest someday.

Any remaining errors or formatting inconsistencies are mine alone. While others generously offered their thoughtful support throughout the process, I handled the final editing and layout—so if anything slipped through, that's on me.

—Nick Allison
Editor, *Record of Dissent*

About The Chaos Section Poetry Project

The Chaos Section Poetry Project is an offshoot of *The Chaos Section*, a long-running opinion site founded in Austin, Texas, in 2012. The poetry side began as a space for work that didn't fit into essays—pieces that were more emotional than argumentative, more fragmented than structured.

Record of Dissent is our first published collection. We may release more in the future.

We're publishing this collection—and any future poetry or prose releases—under the name *The Chaos Section Press*.

For updates or to submit work for future issues, visit:
thechaossectionpoetryproject.com

Vox Poesis Est Vox Libertatis

In the DIY, community spirit of The Chaos Section Poetry Project, this page is intentionally left blank—for you to write your own protest poem. Because your voice belongs in the Record of Dissent, too.

www.ingramcontent.com/pod-product-compliance
Lightning Source LLC
Chambersburg PA
CBHW051639120626
46551CB00014B/2132